Drawing Imaginary Creatures

Level One

Name

Date

D0514636

To parents
Guide your child to write his or her name and date in the box above. Do the exercise along with your child if he or she has difficulty. Throughout this book, you may wish to offer your child a choice of markers, crayons, or colored pencils.

■ Look at each sample. Then trace the lines in each picture below.

fairy

elf

■ Trace the lines. Then color each picture.

■ Trace the lines. Draw the eyes, nose, and mouth. Then color.

Drawing Imaginary Creatures
Level Two

Name

Date

To parents
Encourage your child to use the sample as a guide if he or she has difficulty.

■ Look at each sample. Then trace the lines in each picture below.

witch

Frankenstein

■ Trace the lines. Then color each picture.

■ Trace the lines. Draw the eyes, nose, and mouth. Then color.

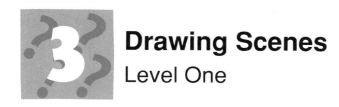

Drawing Scenes
Level One

Name

Date

To parents
Your child may find this activity more difficult because the picture is now more detailed. Encourage him or her to use the sample as a guide. Colored pencils may work best for tracing the lines in these pictures.

■ Look at the sample. Then trace the white lines in the picture below.

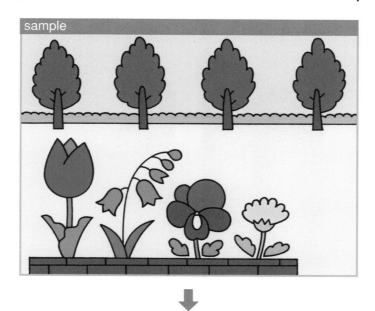

■ Trace the lines. Then color the picture.

■ Draw and color flowers.

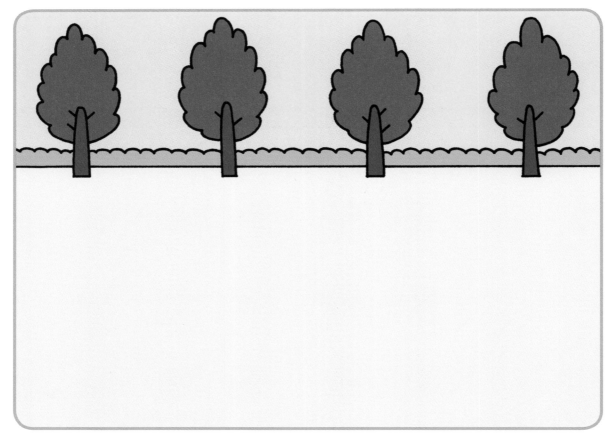

Drawing Scenes
Level Two

Name

Date

To parents
If your child has difficulty, ask him or her to describe the objects in the picture before drawing. It is okay if your child wishes to use different colors from those shown in the sample.

■ Look at the sample. Then trace the white lines in the picture below.

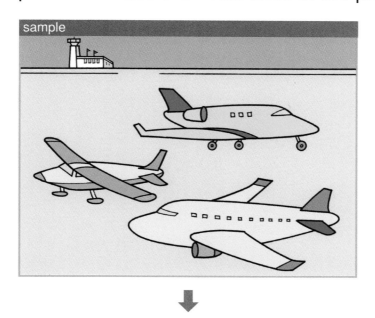

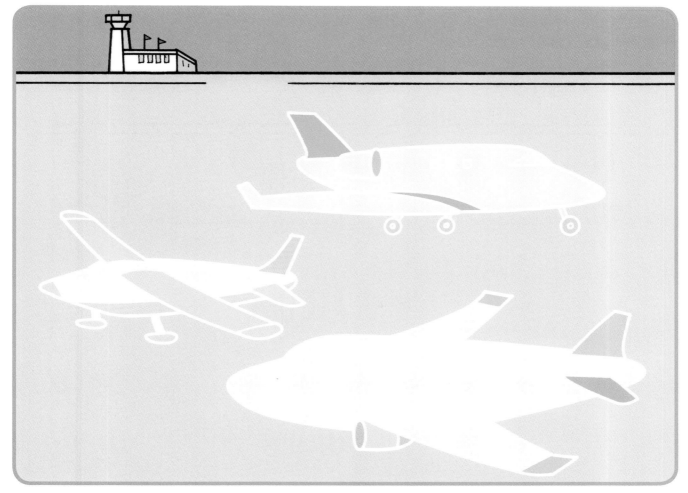

■ Trace the lines. Then color the picture.

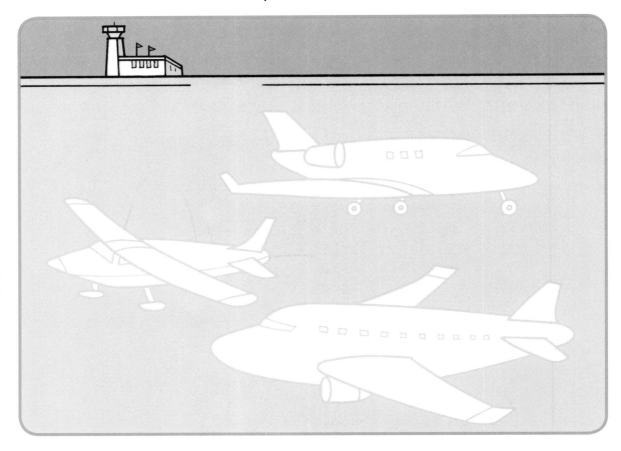

■ Draw and color airplanes.

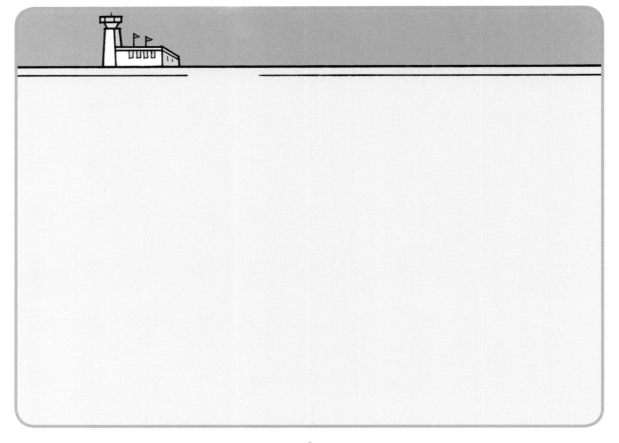

Completing Scenes
Level One

Name

Date

To parents
In this activity, your child will start drawing objects that are different from those shown in the sample.

■ Look at the sample. Then trace the white lines in the picture below.

sample

■ Trace the lines. Then color the picture.

■ Draw two butterflies that are different from the sample. Trace the lines. Then color.

Completing Scenes
Level Two

Name

Date

To parents
As your child progresses through these activities, he or she may start to rely less on the samples and more on his or her own creativity.

■ Look at the sample. Then trace the gray lines in the picture below.

sample

11

■ Trace the lines. Then color.

■Draw a cup and cake that are different from the sample. Trace the lines. Then color.

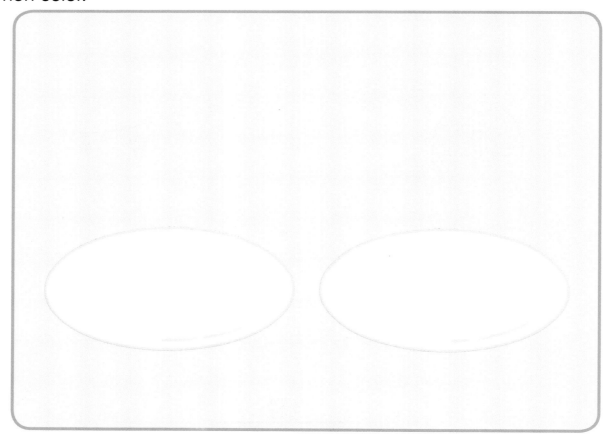

Completing Scenes
Level Three

Name

Date

To parents
When your child has finished, ask your child to describe the decorations he or she has drawn.

■ Look at the sample. Then trace the white lines in the picture below.

13

■ Trace the lines. Then color.

■ Draw three decorations that are different from the sample. Trace the lines.
  Then color.

Completing Scenes
Level Four

Name

Date

To parents
Offer your child a lot of praise for his or her drawing. This will help build your child's confidence in his or her creative abilities.

■ Look at the sample. Then trace the gray lines in the picture below.

■ Trace the lines. Then color.

■ Draw three animals that are different from the sample. Then color.

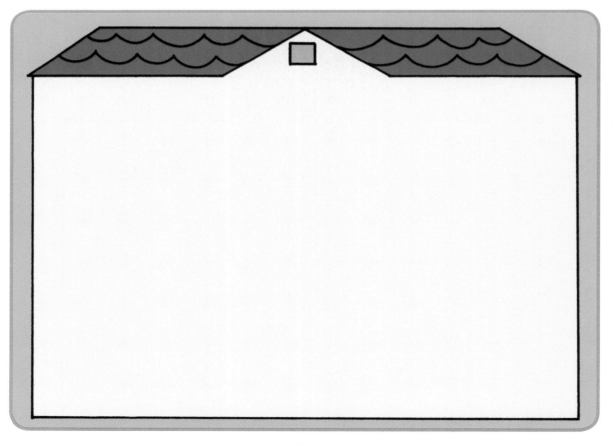

Creative Drawing with Samples

Level One

Name

Date

■ Look at the samples. Draw a beard or mustache on the face. Then trace and color.

To parents
Your child can copy one of the samples or draw something different.

■ Look at the samples. Draw hair on the head. Then trace and color.

Creative Drawing with Samples

Level Two

Name

Date

■ Look at the samples. Draw hair on the head. Then trace and color.

To parents
If your child has difficulty, encourage him or her to use the samples as a guide.

19

■ Look at the samples. Draw ribbons on the hair. Then trace and color.

Creative Drawing
with Samples
Level Three

Name

Date

■ Look at the samples. Draw a baseball cap on the head. Then trace and color.

To parents
Your child's drawing does not need to look like the samples. The samples are provided only as a model.

■ Look at the samples. Draw a pattern on the skirt. Then trace and color.

Creative Drawing with Samples

Level Four

Name

Date

■ Look at the samples. Draw a pattern on the shirt and pants. Then trace and color.

■ Look at the samples. Draw a pattern on the dress. Then trace and color.

Creative Drawing with Samples

Level Five

Name

Date

To parents
From this page on, your child can choose his or her favorite illustrations from the sample.

■ Look at the sample. Then draw and color three piles of blocks of your choice.

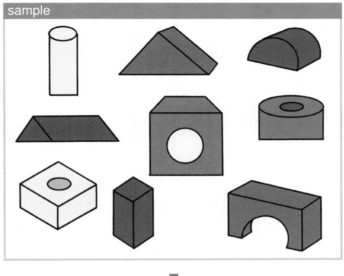

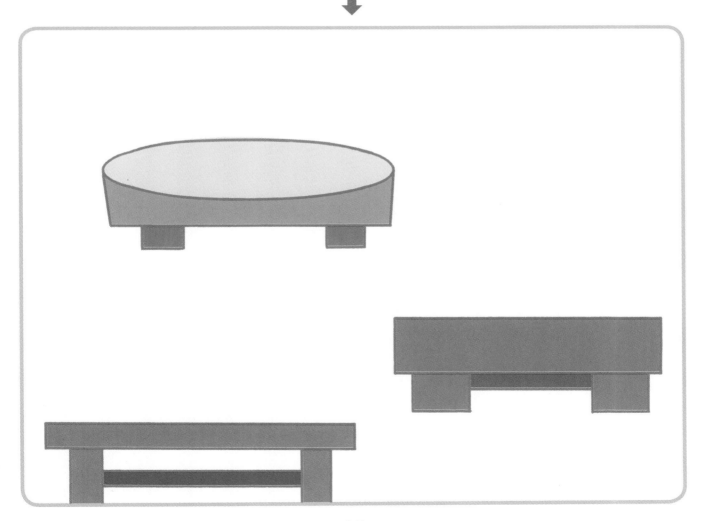

■ Look at the sample. Then draw and color three cakes of your choice.

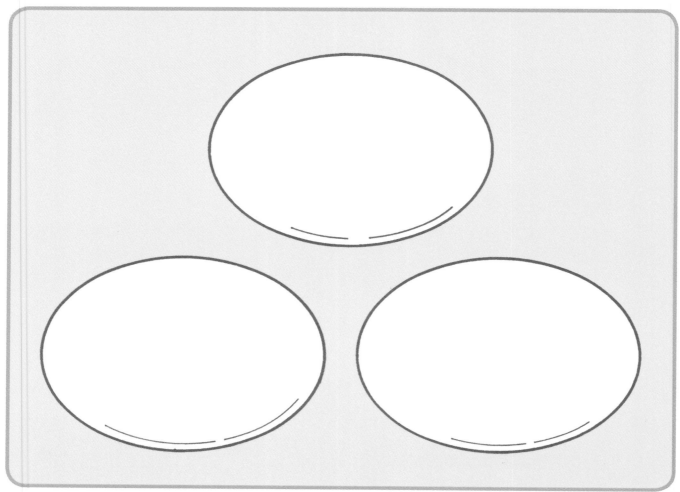

Creative Drawing with Samples

Level Six

Name

Date

To parents
It is okay if your child wishes to use different colors from those shown in the sample.

■ Look at the sample. Then draw and color three flowers of your choice.

sample

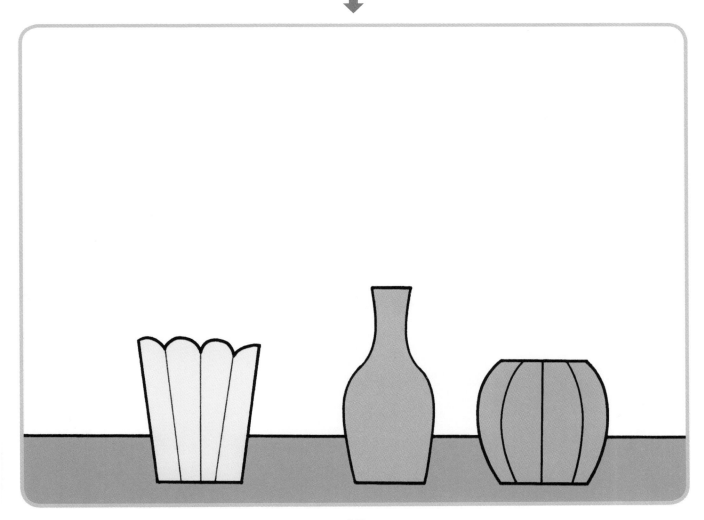

27

■ Look at the sample. Then draw and color three toy cars of your choice.

sample

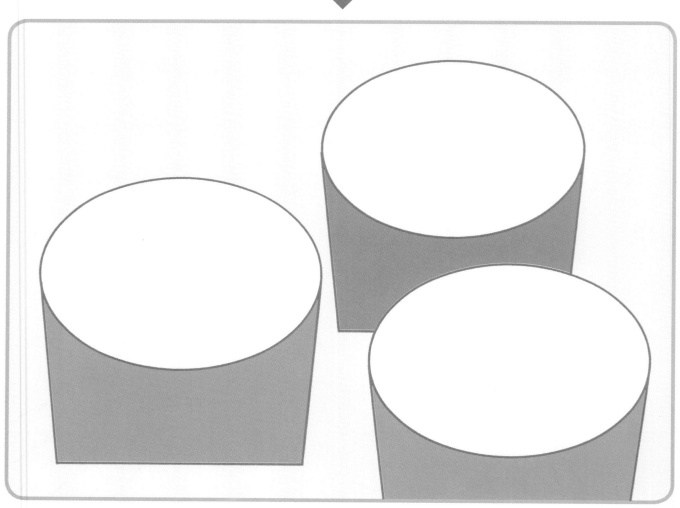

Creative Drawing with Samples

Level Seven

Name

Date

To parents
If your child has difficulty choosing which insects to draw, you can ask your child to pick his or her favorites.

■ Look at the sample. Then draw and color three insects of your choice.

sample

■ Look at the sample. Then draw and color three items of your choice.

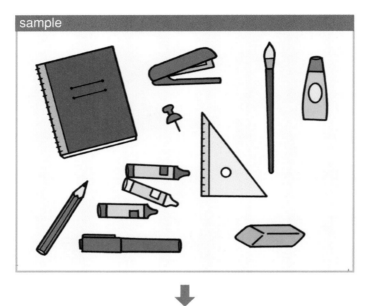

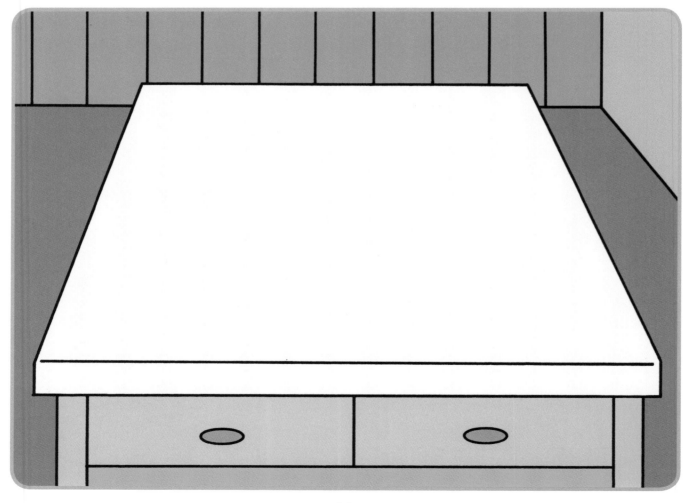

Creative Drawing with Samples

Level Eight

Name

Date

To parents
When your child has finished, ask your child what he or she likes best about his or her drawing.

■ Look at the sample. Then draw and color three fish of your choice.

sample

■ Look at the sample. Then draw and color three baby animals of your choice.

Creative Drawing with Samples

Level Nine

Name

Date

To parents
Encourage your child to enjoy completing the scene by drawing and coloring.

■ Draw and color food on the plates. Then complete the scene as you like.

samples

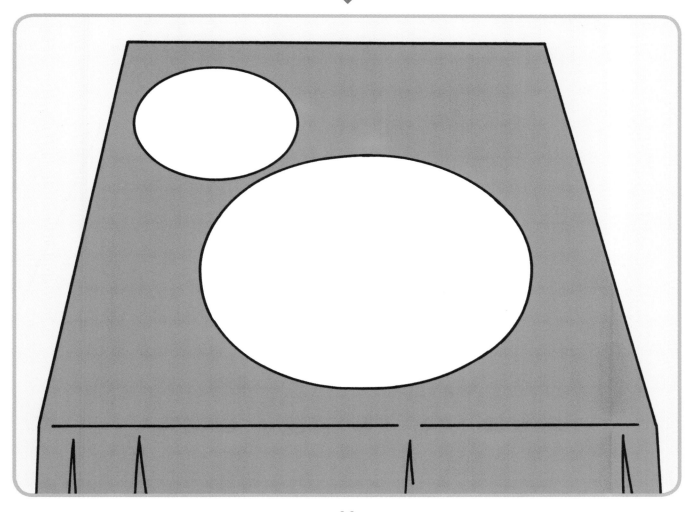

■ Draw and color toys in the room. Then complete the scene as you like.

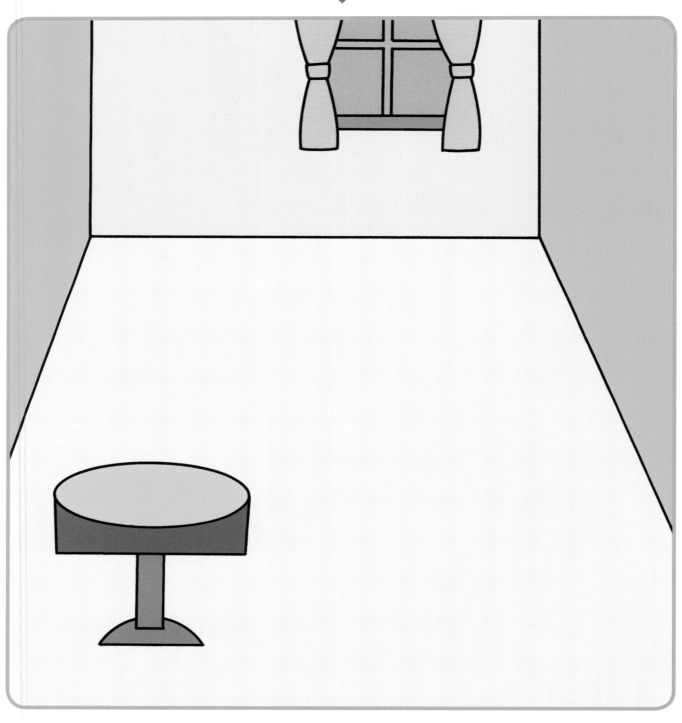

Creative Drawing with Samples

Level Ten

Name

Date

To parents
The sample pictures are examples only. Your child does not need to copy the samples.

■ Draw and color animals behind the fences. Then complete the scene as you like.

samples

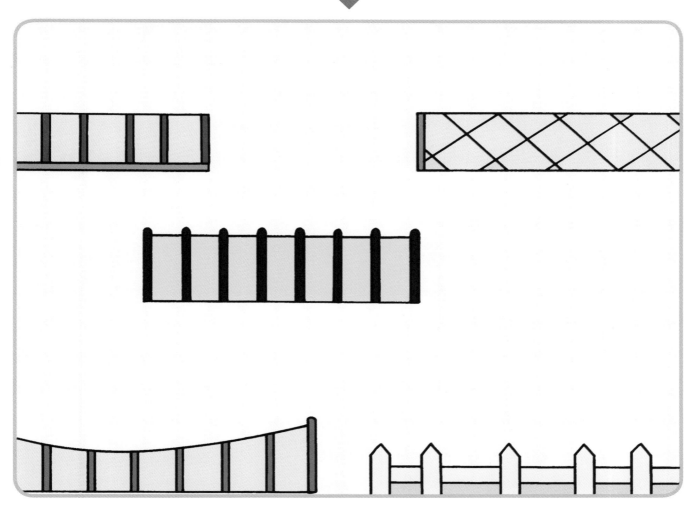

■ Draw and color ghosts and monsters in the party room. Then complete the scene as you like.

samples

Creative Drawing with Samples
Level Eleven

To parents
Guide your child to create a scene by drawing and coloring.

■ Draw and color items in the bedroom. Then complete the scene as you like.

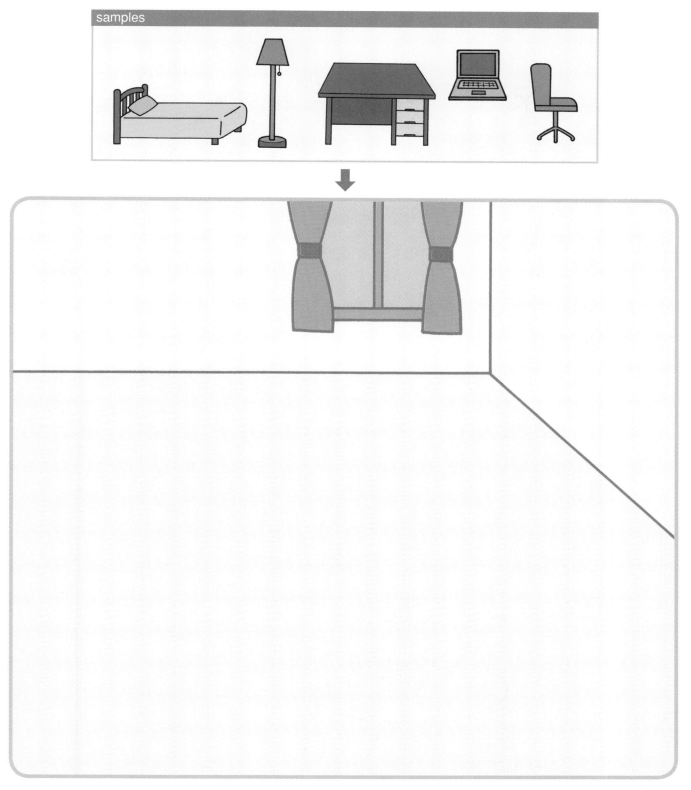

samples

■ Draw and color cars on the highway. Then complete the scene as you like.

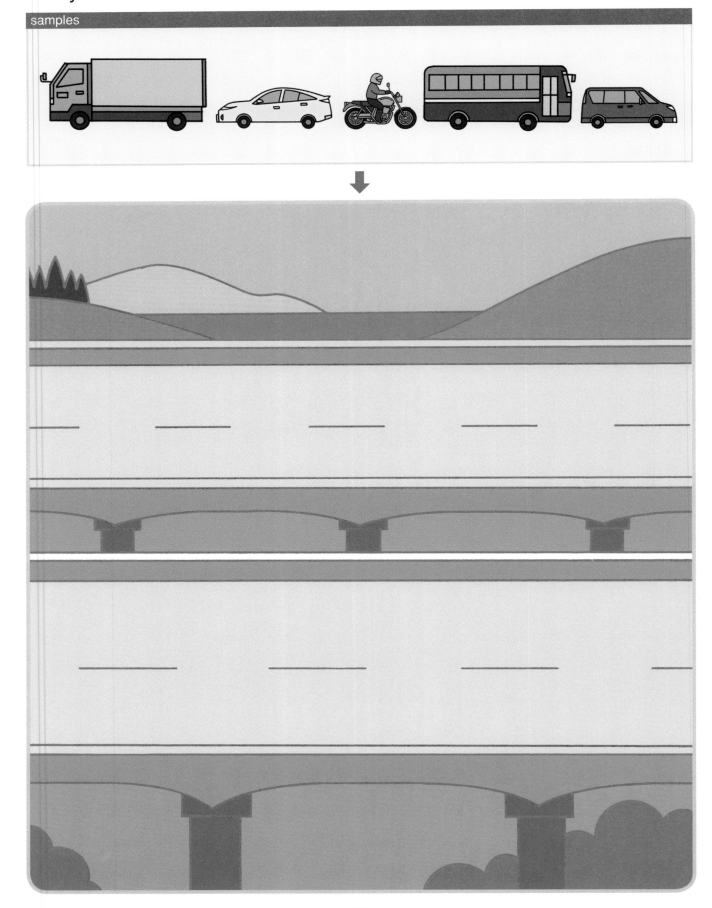

samples

Creative Drawing with Samples

Level Twelve

Name

Date

To parents
Offer your child a lot of praise for his or her drawing. This will help build your child's confidence in his or her creative abilities.

■ Draw and color birds and aircraft in the sky. Then complete the scene as you like.

samples

■ Draw and color plants and animals in the jungle. Then complete the scene as you like.

samples

Creative Drawing
Level One

Name

Date

■ Draw and color fireworks in the sky.

To parents
From this page on, no samples are provided. You may wish to read the directions out loud to your child. For this page, crayons work best for drawing fireworks.

■ Draw and color a field of flowers.

Creative Drawing
Level Two

Name

Date

■ Draw and color animals in a fish tank.

To parents
Your child can draw and color the background if he or she wants.

■ Draw and color fashion models in a fashion show.

Creative Drawing
Level Three

Name

Date

■ Draw and color people and buildings in a city.

To parents
Guide your child to draw and color a picture related to the topic.

Draw and color stormy weather on a mountain.

Creative Drawing
Level Four

Name

Date

■ Draw and color children playing outside on a winter day.

To parents
If your child has difficulty, ask your child to first describe what he or she wants to draw.

■ Draw and color an amusement park.

Creative Drawing with Sample Pictures
Level One

Name

Date

■ Draw and color a dog. You can use the sample pictures to help you.

To parents
From this page on, two photographs are provided as samples. Your child does not need to try to copy the samples. Also, your child can draw more than one animal if he or she wants.

■Draw and color a cat. You can use the sample pictures to help you.

Creative Drawing
with Sample Pictures
Level Two

Name
Date

■ Draw and color a rabbit. You can use the sample pictures to help you.

To parents
Your child can draw and color the background if he or she wants.

■ Draw and color an insect. You can use the sample pictures to help you.

Creative Drawing with Sample Pictures

Level Three

Name

Date

■ Draw and color a bird. You can use the sample pictures to help you.

To parents
Your child does not need to complete an entire scene. It is okay if your child just wants to draw and color an animal.

53

■Draw and color a bird. You can use the sample pictures to help you.

Creative Drawing
with Sample Pictures
Level Four

Name

Date

■ Draw and color an ape. You can use the sample pictures to help you.

To parents
When your child has finished, ask your child to describe what he or she has drawn.

56

■ Draw and color a flower. You can use the sample pictures to help you.

Creative Drawing
with Sample Pictures
Level Five

Name

Date

■ Draw and color an animal. You can use the sample pictures to help you.

To parents
Encourage your child to enjoy drawing and coloring.

■ Draw and color an animal. You can use the sample pictures to help you.

Creative Drawing with Sample Pictures

Level Six

■ Draw and color an animal. You can use the sample pictures to help you.

To parents
Offer your child a lot of praise for his or her drawing. This will help build your child's confidence in his or her creative abilities.

■ Draw and color an animal. You can use the sample pictures to help you.

Creative Drawing
Level One

Name

Date

■ Draw and color your favorite food.

To parents
From this page on, neither samples nor background colors are provided. You may wish to read the directions out loud to your child.

What is your favorite food?

■ Draw and color your favorite animal.

What is your favorite animal?

Creative Drawing
Level Two

Name

Date

■ Draw and color your favorite flower.

To parents
Guide your child to draw and color anything he or she wishes, as long as it fits the topic.

What is your favorite flower?

64

■ Draw and color your favorite kind of vehicle.

what is your favorite kind of vehicle?

Creative Drawing
Level Three

Name

Date

■ Draw and color your favorite moment in a book.

To parents
When your child has finished, ask your child what he or she has drawn. Talk about the book with your child.

What is your favorite moment in a book?

■Draw and color your best friends.

who are your best friends?

Creative Drawing
Level Four

Name

Date

■ Draw and color your family.

To parents
If your child has difficulty, have him or her describe each family member before drawing.

Ask your family to be your models!

■ Draw and color your favorite activity.

What is your favorite activity?

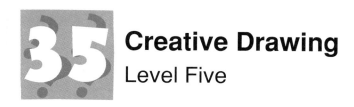

Creative Drawing
Level Five

■ Draw and color one exciting thing you did last summer.

To parents
When your child has finished, ask your child what he or she has drawn. Talk about the summer activity with your child.

What was one exciting thing you did last summer?

■ Draw and color your favorite memory of Halloween.

What is your favorite memory of Halloween?

Creative Drawing
Level Six

- Draw and color the best meal you have ever had.

To parents
If your child has difficulty, reviewing the previous pages may help him or her get ideas.

What was the best meal you have ever had?

To parents
This is the last exercise of this workbook. Please praise your child for the effort it took to complete this workbook.

■ Draw and color your favorite memory from a family trip.

what is your favorite memory from a family trip?

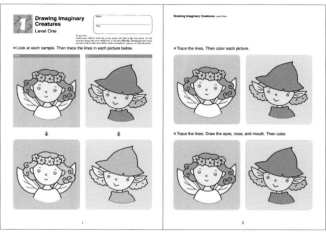

pages 1 and 2

pages 3 and 4

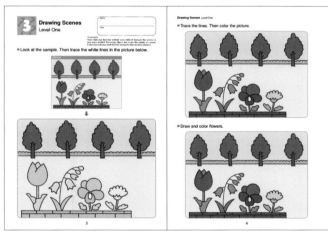

pages 5 and 6

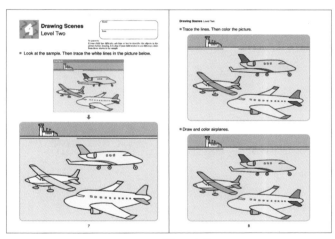

pages 7 and 8

pages 9 and 10

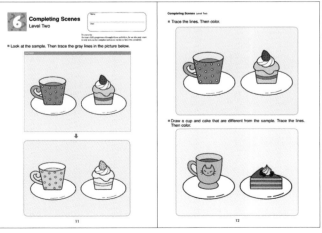

pages 11 and 12

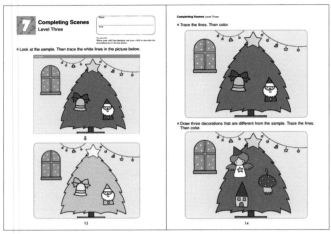

pages 13 and 14

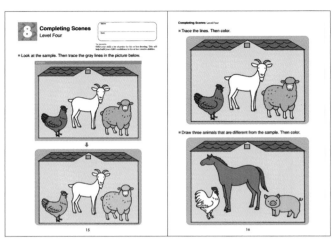

pages 15 and 16

pages 17 and 18

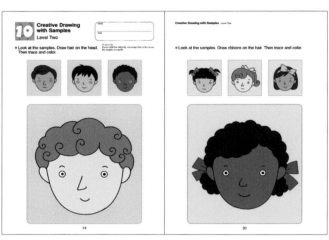

pages 19 and 20

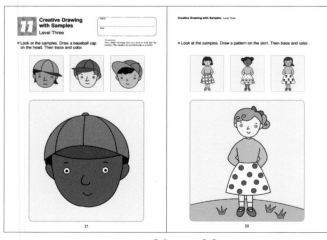

pages 21 and 22

pages 23 and 24

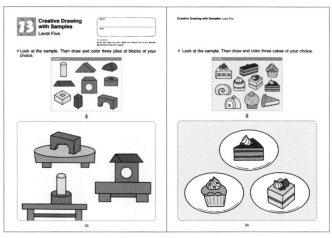

pages 25 and 26

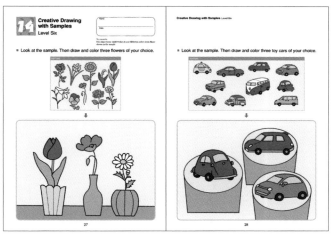

pages 27 and 28

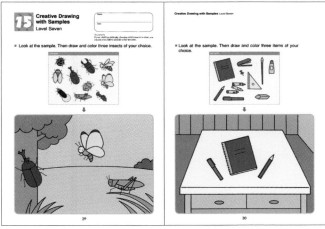

pages 29 and 30

pages 31 and 32

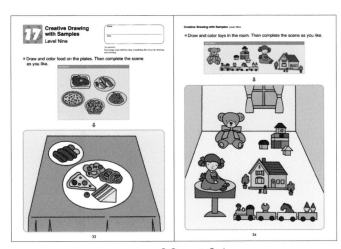

pages 33 and 34

pages 35 and 36

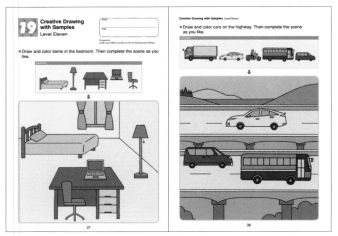

pages 37 and 38

pages 39 and 40

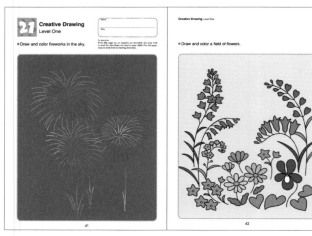

pages 41 and 42

pages 43 and 44

pages 45 and 46

pages 47 and 48

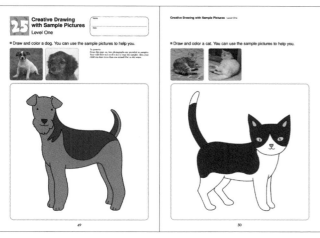

pages 49 and 50

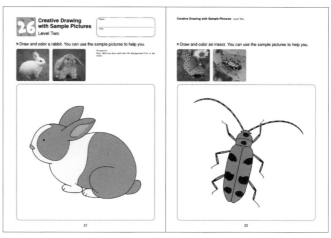

pages 51 and 52

pages 53 and 54

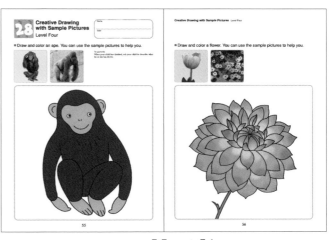

pages 55 and 56

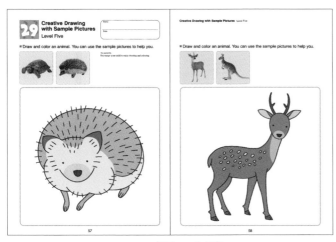

pages 57 and 58

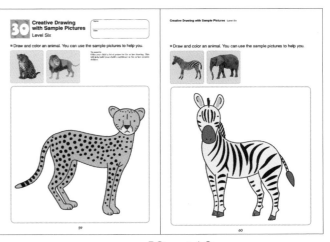

pages 59 and 60

pages 61 and 62

pages 63 and 64

pages 65 and 66

pages 67 and 68

pages 69 and 70

pages 71 and 72

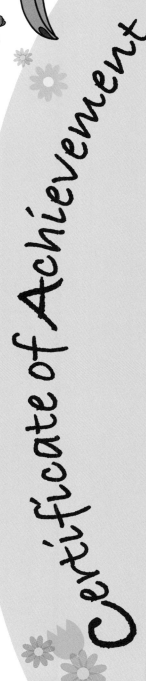

Certificate of Achievement

....

is hereby congratulated on completing

Thinking Skills Workbooks
Kindergarten Creativity

Presented on .... , 20 ....

....

Parent or Guardian

KUM○N